Meditation

An Introductory Guide To Meditation: Alleviating Stress, Anxiety, And Depression To Embrace A State Of Inner Serenity And Joy

(How To Attain Physical Relaxation And Cultivate Inner Tranquility Through The Practice Of Meditation)

Gilbert Joyce

TABLE OF CONTENT

Mindfulness Meditation..1

Stress Is A Significant Concern In Contemporary Society..12

Troubleshooting Meditation Problems..............41

Meditation As Therapy..52

Methods For Initiating The Relaxation Process 60

The Dispositions Of Felicity And Appreciation 69

Sleep Anxiety Management Through The Application Of Directed Hypnosis Methodologies 80

Important Considerations While Meditating..86

The Benefits Of Meditation 102

Varieties Of Meditation Practices To Employ At Present..109

Commencing The Day & Establishing A Purpose 119

Clare's Ten Effortless Strategies For Meditation 134

Introduction To Various Forms Of Meditation Suitable For Novices.. 139

Varieties And Methods Of Meditation 146

What Is Mindfulness? 159

Mindfulness Meditation

Mindfulness Meditation Techniques have been derived from conventional Buddhist meditation practices and bear a striking resemblance to Zen meditation. These techniques involve the concentrated concentration on one's breath and the cultivation of a state of being solely present in the current moment.

There exists no stipulation for the involvement of conscious thoughts; the procedure pertains to the cognizance of one's physical and mental state, as well as the observation of one's surroundings.

When initiating the practice of mindfulness meditation, one will observe an inherent propensity for being susceptible to distractions. This form of diversion necessitates recognition and necessitates the redirection of focus towards one's breath.

This practice cultivates the mental capacity to direct your attention to an encompassing consciousness of all the elements present in that particular moment. You will be attuned not only to the audial reception of verbal communication, but will also actively engage in the art of attentive listening. Your consciousness will be attuned to observe and assimilate the presence of individuals, flora, fauna, and the like in your immediate surroundings, while simultaneously maintaining focused attention on your primary objective at that moment.

In contemporary society, we allocate a significant portion of our time operating on automatic mode, thus frequently failing to sensitize ourselves to the essence of existence. This meditation practice will cultivate a state of complete mental awareness.

It may be considered one of the most accessible techniques for those new to meditation; nevertheless, attaining mastery of this level of awareness will require consistent dedication and a significant investment of time.

Compassionate Meditation

This methodology is derived from the Tibetan Buddhist tradition and is grounded in the principles of compassion and universal empathy.

The practice necessitates the individual to assume a seated position with closed eyes, directing their attention towards cultivating emotions of benevolence and empathy. This process commences by directing these feelings towards oneself, before expanding them outwardly to encompass all beings and the entirety of existence.

The cultivation of visualization is a valuable ability to foster while engaging in compassionate meditation, proving particularly efficacious for individuals grappling with low self-esteem, insomnia, negative cognitive patterns, anxiety and depression, as well as those contending with anger-related concerns.

Mantra Meditation

This technique proves to be highly efficacious for individuals facing difficulties in practicing breath-focused meditation. Throughout centuries, adherents of Hinduism, Sikhism, Buddhism, and numerous other cultures and religions have employed it.

Rather than placing the mind's attention on the act of breathing, one can engage in the repetitive recitation of a mantra. (Some cultural traditions employ this technique in conjunction with the emphasis on breath regulation.)

The incessant repetition, whether spoken aloud or internalized, compels you to disengage from extraneous thoughts as you concentrate on the act of chanting.

It is commonly held that the consistent recitation of a mantra induces vibrations that enable the mind to attain heightened levels of consciousness.

An individual who has acquired considerable expertise in this particular method of meditation may experience a gradual dissipation of the chant, giving way to an elevated state of consciousness.

Certain customs involve the utilization of prayer beads to assist with the recitation of mantras. These beads are typically characterized by their elongated structure and consist of a total of 108 beads. While various conjectures exist concerning the rationale behind the specific number 108, no conclusive explanation has been discovered throughout my years of diligent exploration. However, it is widely accepted that all these theories revolve around the notion of its profound spiritual connotation.

Every bead is tallied as the mantra is iterated, and the number of repetitions can correspondingly vary based on the duration of your meditation.

If you are inclined to engage in Mantra Meditation and have a preference for employing beads, I would suggest crafting your own set in order to imbue them with a sense of personal significance.

You will need:

A substantial thread, preferably made of cotton due to its natural properties, although any durable and slender string or cord will suffice.

A talisman to symbolize the intended focus of the contemplation.

Beads – a maximum of 108, although you may choose to use a number that is most suitable to your personal preference and comfort level.

It is not necessary to possess beads that are perfectly identical, however, it is advised to adhere to a color scheme that aligns with your intended meditative purpose.

Securely fasten a knot at one end of the string before carefully stringing the beads. After threading all the beads, it is recommended to leave a small surplus of string before securely fastening the two ends together and subsequently attaching the charm.

Various colors are linked to distinct forms of meditation:

Purple symbolizes the expansion of one's spiritual development and heightened consciousness.

Blue is often associated with the concepts of healing, fostering friendships, cultivating peace, and instilling hope.

Red is associated with confidence, as well as inner strength and courage.

Green is associated with concepts such as fertility, financial wealth, the natural world, and the planet Earth.

Pink is often associated with the expression of affection and the strong bonds within a familial unit.

There exists a plethora of ancient mantras available for utilization; however, there is no rationale for precluding the option to select one's own mantra. The paramount factor to consider when making a personal choice is its relevance to oneself.

Ancient Mantras

'Om' – Om, also known as Ohm, is widely regarded as the sonic manifestation of the cosmos, the primordial resonance that emanates from our planet. It embodies the perpetual nature of existence, encompassing the stages of birth, demise, and subsequent renewal.

I offer my humble reverence to Lord Ganesh, the divine being characterized by his elephant visage, known for his immense ability to eliminate any impediments. I kindly request for blessings and safeguarding."

'Om Mani Padme Hum' - A Tibetan Buddhist Mantra signifying reverence for the Jewel residing within the Lotus

I pay homage to the sacred essence residing within my being, using the invocation 'Om Namah Shivaya'.

Modern Mantras

"Embody the transformation you desire to witness in society" - Mahatma Gandhi

I have the ability to alter my perspectives, consequently shaping the reality that surrounds me.

I am amenable to accepting gifts of a universal nature.

I am capable of accomplishing remarkable feats.

The principles of 'Shanti Veda Prajna' encompass tranquility, intelligence, and sagacity.

Stress Is A Significant Concern In Contemporary Society.

The prevailing understanding amongst individuals is that the profound issue of our era - stress - is inherently linked to feelings of existential purposelessness, estrangement, and discontentment.

Stress is not an innovation of contemporary society. Early humans encountered various forms of distress, albeit within the context of relatively uncomplicated life circumstances that diverged significantly from the complexities of contemporary stressors. He engaged in frequent movement, thereby mitigating the impacts of stress, consequently allowing him to experience prolonged relaxation whilst seated beside the campfire. Typically, he enjoyed additional opportunities for repose, as once various tasks were accomplished, he returned to a more tranquil state, which was comparably less burdensome than that of contemporary individuals. Currently, a considerable number of individuals find themselves in a prolonged state of suspense, thereby severely restricting their capacity for relaxation.

Approximately 33% of individuals report experiencing impaired sleep, often attributed to psychological factors. And all due to the daily burden predominantly linked to emotional encounters - anxiety, ambiguity, occupational discontent, dissatisfaction with one's existence. In the case of primitive individuals, stress predominantly revolved around physical constraints such as temperature extremes, inadequate sustenance, and similar challenges. Over the past century, there has been a shift in the source of stress from the physical realm to the domain of the mind.

The stress response of an individual is determined less by the tense situations themselves, and more by their personal evaluation of the threat inherent in those situations. At times, you may desire and possess the capability to handle any forthcoming predicament autonomously. This is applicable when you are able to achieve restful sleep, maintain equilibrium, and enjoy positive disposition amidst favorable weather conditions. However, the scenario alters on days where difficulties arise due to a less auspicious start.

Individuals are subjected to both physical and psychological strain without receiving adequate recompense in the form of relaxation and tranquility as opposed to a state of agitation. If an individual is unable to unwind, they consistently experience the sensation of being a tightly wound clockwork mechanism. The capacity for profound relaxation - the paramount element in fostering a state of well-being and contentment. The primary inquiry revolves around the means through which this can be accomplished.

Mindful Contemplation - an Effortless Remedy

Meditation offers an unparalleled blend of fortitude and tranquility, making it the most exceptional means of rejuvenation. In order to fully unlock our intellectual, physical, and spiritual capacities, it is crucial for us to employ a comprehensive approach encompassing profound rest, relaxation, and inner dialogue. In its absence, our capacity to employ our genuine capabilities is merely marginal. Meditation serves as a transformative means of self-discovery and self-renewal, irrespective of our circumstances and the various challenges we encounter in our daily lives. Meditation offers a straightforward means to address all concerns and promote the restoration of physical well-being.

The inherent cognitive ability of individuals to engage in meditative practices

Extensive contemplation in contemporary times demonstrates that inherent ability for meditation exists within all individuals. The practice of meditation is an inherent and innate capacity possessed by all individuals. The automatic process of relaxation of body and mind is activated whenever there is an occasion to attain tranquility. Meditative techniques harness this inherent mechanism of relaxation and utilize it to induce a state of calm. Over time, both the physical and mental aspects acclimate to achieving a state of relaxation regardless of the circumstances, thereby harmoniously merging with periods of rest and engagement. To regain this capability and cultivate it, one must simply identify the appropriate course of action.

When conversing with Li Shan, an esteemed American authority on meditation, one can express the concept that meditation serves as a means to reclaim and rediscover a state or possession that may have been lost, albeit with a sense of uncertainty regarding its nature, whereabouts, and timing. This can potentially invigorate your intrinsic faculties and effectively augment your capacity for affection, your exuberance, zeal, and perspective in recognizing your interconnectedness with the cosmos, ensuring that you remain forever integrated and indistinguishable from it. Furthermore, it has the potential to enhance one's capacity to navigate proficiently in various aspects of daily existence."

1

Developing a Proficient Devotional Practice

Is conducted discreetly" or "Is executed behind closed doors

Jesus instructed, "When you engage in the act of prayer, withdraw into the solitude of your private chamber, and once you have secured the privacy of your surroundings, direct your supplications to your heavenly Father, who resides in the concealed realm. Rest assured that your unseen Father shall openly bestow his blessings upon you" (Matthew 6:6, King James Version).

Initially, I comprehended this excerpt as necessitating my withdrawal into a secluded setting with the intent of engaging in conversation with the divine. I have come to the understanding that the closet serves as a form of meditation. Close the entrance to the external realm. Close your mind to the distractions arising from the external realm. Remain sufficiently tranquil to receive communication from the Father. The psalmist made mention that God possesses a concealed sanctuary. In times of adversity, I shall find refuge within his pavilion; concealed within the sacred confines of his tabernacle, I shall be shielded. He will exalt me upon an unyielding foundation. Within this earthly abode, there exists a designated space, a concealed refuge, a clandestine alcove meticulously arranged by the Patron. Upon encountering the Father in that place, we may attain a profound tranquility that surpasses the grasp of mortal comprehension.

We must maintain a state of tranquility and composure in order to transcend the incessant clamor and diversions. Jesus stated, "Indeed, your Father is aware of your needs even prior to your supplication" (Matthew 6:8, New International Version). We must be still and listen. This practice traces back to the ancestral heritage predating the arrival of our predecessors on the American shores in a state of captivity.

I must emphasize that the act of engaging in public prayer is appropriate within specific contexts. We need public prayer. It is necessary for us to partake in the recitation of the Lord's Prayer. It is imperative for us to listen to the supplications of the devout and virtuous individuals. Considerable knowledge can be gained by attentively observing an individual engage in the act of prayer.

Upon commencing my tenure in the clergy, Reverend Dr. Charles L. Dinkins advised me, 'Charles, it would be beneficial for you to commence attending prayer gatherings to nourish your spirit.' During my participation in these prayer meetings, I frequently heard Deacon Lynum and Deacon Washington utter prayers such as, 'Oh Lord, grant me the strength to refrain from reveling in my adversary's ruin or growing conceited in my triumph.' Assist in guiding my adversaries towards a transformation in their behavior. May the individuals fervently seek your divine guidance, O Lord, inquiring sincerely about the actions required for their salvation."

Upon innumerable repetitions of the aforementioned prayer by Brother Lynum and Brother Washington, my comprehension of their professed beliefs was gradually illuminated. I observed the true nature of their character through their handling of opposition. I found it necessary to conduct introspection and analyze my approach in handling opposition. I harbored a fervent wish to seamlessly integrate this prayer into my mode of living and employ it in countering any resistance encountered. Jesus openly prayed, making his words audible to those around him. Public prayer carries merit.

#4: Metta/Loving-Kindness Meditation

In order to cultivate a heightened state of tranquility and contentment, as well as promote overall emotional and mental wellness, it is imperative to engage in a form of meditation that facilitates the development of self-compassion. After all, true happiness stems from embracing and finding satisfaction in one's authentic self. It is essential that you engage in the practice of Metta or Loving Kindness meditation.

Metta meditation is a form of contemplative practice that, not only encompasses the advantages associated with all manner of meditative techniques, but also facilitates the development of profound self-affection, heightened perception, enhanced self-awareness, genuine self-compassion, unshakable self-confidence, and a myriad of other virtuous qualities which, upon integration into one's psyche, contribute to a state of increased overall well-being, reduced anxiety, and liberation from stress.

Metta meditation proves particularly efficacious as a means to foster happiness and alleviate stress and anxiety. Numerous research investigations have conclusively demonstrated that regular engagement in this form of meditation can foster emotional fortitude, aid in the management of anger and emotional regulation challenges, and foster the development of coping strategies necessary for effectively navigating the demands of daily existence with composure and profound tranquility.

Allow me to elucidate the techniques for engaging in the practice of loving-kindness meditation:

How to

"Engage in Metta meditation in the following manner:

Step 1

Allocate dedicated time for regular practice and, as previously mentioned, opt for practicing in a serene environment, at least temporarily. With consistent practice, your capacity to engage in "meditation" in less favorable surroundings will enhance.

Set your timer to a session of ideal length depending on how the time you've curved out for the practice, adopt an ideal posture—you can sit, lie down, or use any other comfortable posture—and relax by practicing breath mindfulness meditation for several minutes.

Step 2

By directing your attention to the observation of your breath in the present moment, you will experience a tranquil state of mind. Similar to the nature of many meditation practices, it is inevitable that thoughts will arise as you observe your breath and immerse yourself in its current magnificence. Let them.

It is imperative to bear in mind that a state of meditation can be achieved by maintaining a high level of attentiveness, be it towards the current moment or a specific object, to the extent that one can discern whenever the mind veers away from its intended focal point. Engaging in this activity with increasing frequency will result in a heightened ability to focus on deliberate mindfulness and meticulous observance of a singular subject.

As you gradually experience a sense of tranquility and heightened mindfulness, endeavor to construct a vivid depiction of your current state of being. Devote your attention to your exceptional favorable qualities of character and express gratitude towards yourself for the individual that you have become, encompassing flaws, errors, obstacles, and every aspect; engage in this practice briefly.

As you gradually embrace a profound sense of tranquility, express compassionate and benevolent thoughts towards yourself either silently within your mind or articulating them audibly. For example, one could express these sentiments as follows: "I am filled with joy, I am serenely calm, and I am in a state of good health and well-being." If you are currently experiencing a lack of happiness or freedom from stress, an alternative approach would be to express these desirable sentiments towards oneself (and others) through the formulation of phrases such as, 'may

I attain a state of ____ (happiness, security, tranquility, emotional strength, achievement, serenity,' and the like.

Step 3

As you utter these words, allow them to serve as your focal point. Delight in the significance they hold, the compassionate and self-affirming essence they embody, and their inherent warmth. In the event that your thoughts wander, observe this occurrence, acknowledge it, and kindly redirect your attention back to your chosen loving-kindness thought or sentiment. Embrace the emotions that arise from these sentiments and allow them to envelop you.

Maintain a steadfast focus on cultivating your loving-kindness mindset throughout the entirety of your session. Additionally, you may engage in the practice of Metta meditation while directing your attention towards the well-being of others. As previously indicated, a concrete illustration of expressing affection and benevolence towards one's cherished individuals can be observed. It simply entails uttering phrases such as "May my mother, aunt, spouse, offspring, companion, and all others..." Embrace a state of tranquility and affection.

Incorporating daily Metta meditation into your daily regimen will amplify your capacity for self-love and self-acknowledgment. As a result of this, you will cultivate an elevated capacity to cultivate self-awareness, self-compassion, and self-esteem, leading to an increased emotional fortitude and adeptness in gracefully maneuvering through the numerous obstacles encountered in contemporary society.

Beginners First Step

Are you familiar with the practice of meditation and its potential positive impact on both your physical and mental well-being, prompting you to consider incorporating it into your routine? Regrettably, you find yourself lacking precise knowledge on where to commence, how to execute it, and where to proceed. This chapter provides comprehensive coverage on the topic. You will gain knowledge of the fundamental concepts necessary to initiate the endeavor.

A recommended initial step to embark on the practice of meditation is to conduct thorough research on the subject matter. Please refrain from initiating a venture unless you possess a clear understanding of its ultimate destination and the means by which you shall reach it. Initiating the practice of meditation without due consideration of pertinent knowledge and guidance is a primary factor contributing to the phenomenon whereby numerous individuals commence their endeavors with great enthusiasm, yet cease their involvement soon thereafter.

In order to acquire a more profound comprehension of meditation, it is imperative to address the following inquiries:

• What is meditation?

• What is the historical lineage of meditation?

- What are the advantages of practicing meditation? • What are the positive effects of engaging in meditation? • What are the merits of incorporating meditation into one's daily routine?

- Can you please elaborate on the mechanisms and processes involved in meditation?

- How are meditation, posture, the mind, and the necessity to concentrate interconnected?

- What is the duration required to engage in practice?

- What methods can I employ to ascertain and quantify the advantages? • How can I effectively discern and evaluate the merits? • In what manner can I perceive and assess the benefits?

- Can you please elucidate the distinctions between meditation, relaxation, concentration, and focusing?

- Does mediation have any correlation with Yoga?

- Is it appropriate for individuals of the Muslim, Christian, and other faiths to engage in meditation?

- What is the recommended duration for your meditation practice – is it meant to be a lifelong commitment, or is it typically advised for a shorter period of a few months or years?

- What would be the consequences of discontinuing your meditation practice after it has already been commenced?

- What is the proper method for practicing meditation?

Nonetheless, delving extensively into the vast expanse of meditation literature is not imperative; rather, a rudimentary understanding of meditation essentials would suffice. Once you have acquired this information, you will find it considerably easier to acquire mastery of the technique and advance. The subsequent elucidation comprises the fundamental aspects of meditation intended to acquaint novices.

Locate a designated area

The optimal location for engaging in meditation is in a serene environment. Select a location within the confines of your residence that affords you a sense of ease and contentment. If you possess an additional room within your abode, that is certainly permissible. However, should your dwelling be constricted in terms of available space, it would be prudent to select one of the corners within an existing room. Regard your chosen location as a sanctified space for personal exploration; in doing so, your cognitive and emotional faculties will consistently react as you tread upon its grounds. In order to create a more revitalizing ambiance, it is suggested to furnish the area with a table and drape it with a sheer fabric. Place a vase containing fresh flowers and a lit candle upon the table. If you feel at ease with the act of kindling incense, then proceed accordingly. Through the deliberate enhancement of the ambiance, an environment conducive to meditation can be established.

Prepare physically

While the focus of meditation lies predominantly on internal aspects, it is important to acknowledge the significance of our physical appearance as well. "When engaging in the preparation for meditation, one may undertake the following actions:

- Engage in personal hygiene by taking a shower. Alternatively, if the scheduling does not permit, opt to cleanse your hands and face.

- Opt for lightweight clothing and loose-fitting garments to enhance your comfort.

- Remove your shoes. It is advisable to give your feet respite as well.

In order to minimize any potential disruptions, please ensure that all of your electronic devices, including media devices and cell phones, are kept at a considerable distance. It is acceptable to incorporate music into the meditation practice; however, it is crucial to exercise caution in selecting music that does not impede the meditative experience. Music serves as a conduit for the expression of the innermost essence, acting as a means through which proficient practitioners enhance the caliber of their meditative states. Nevertheless, it is imperative to maintain a low volume and refrain from engaging in any form of dancing or singing along to the music.

Choose a suitable timeframe and create an itinerary for engaging in meditation.

If feasible, make an effort to establish a consistent schedule for your daily meditation sessions. One could potentially consider implementing the same principle of regularly scheduling meals into their meditation routine, as one tends to always be conscious of when to have breakfast, lunch, and dinner. Ideally, engage in the act of meditation upon awakening in the morning, as a consequence, an enduring sense of joy and spiritual sustenance shall permeate your being throughout the entirety of the day.

It is also advisable to establish the duration of each meditation session. For beginners, initiating with 10-minute sessions is recommended, gradually progressing to 15-minute durations as proficiency is attained.

Inform those in your proximity

In situations where you intend to engage in home meditation, there may be instances where you will not find yourself in solitude. When one enters into matrimony, they acquire a spouse and offspring, and similarly, residing with one's parents alters the surroundings.

In order to optimize the benefits of mediation and minimize any potential disturbances, kindly inform others of your engagement in meditation and your need for a serene atmosphere.

If you have young children, ensure that they are not present. Nevertheless, if they possess a sufficient level of comprehension, it is advisable to communicate your expectations to them as well.

Practice makes perfect

Meditation is a practice that necessitates mastering in order to attain its advantages. Initially, you may encounter challenges in maintaining a still and concentrated posture while establishing a deep connection with your inner being. As you advance, you will gain the proficiency to practice with ease, comprehend the outcomes, and adeptly modify the surroundings to accommodate your requirements. The most challenging aspect of meditation can lie in the utilization of "Yourself" since you assume the roles of the experiencer, the student, the instructor, the evaluator of one's own progress, and the entity that becomes unveiled.

Lastly, the most robust cornerstone for your meditation practice resides within oneself. It is imperative that you possess a comprehensive understanding of the notion of mediation, foster a constructive mindset, and exhibit a willingness to acquire new knowledge. Please bear in mind that it is essential for one to engage in meditation personally, as it is not possible for another individual to fulfill this practice on your behalf. Fortunately, the procedure is cost-free, uncomplicated, and readily graspable. In the practice of meditation, it is essential to recognize and acknowledge the functions of the mind and the neurons, as this knowledge will enable you to effectively cultivate conscious control over your focus.

If you have recently commenced, or are on the verge of commencing, proceed forth! The task at hand is indeed uncomplicated.

Troubleshooting Meditation Problems

Engaging in meditation can pose difficulties occasionally. This chapter aims to provide you with guidance on how to effectively address and overcome obstacles, enabling you to sustain a consistent routine.

Finding Time to Meditate

Meditating entails dedicating one's time. Select a meditation technique that resonates with you and commit to practicing it consistently. You may initiate the practice of meditation by devoting a minimum of 3 to 5 minutes per day. It is imperative that you engage in the activity on a regular basis in order to cultivate optimal cognitive function. Engaging in meditation on a consistent basis, ideally once or twice daily for the majority of the week, is considered a prudent and rational practice.

Determine the optimal period during the day for engaging in meditation, with a specific focus on identifying a time frame conducive to undivided and dedicated contemplation. This is the time when you are not excessively occupied, fatigued, or diverted. Practicing meditation promptly upon awakening can be highly advantageous due to the comparatively unburdened state of the mind. Prioritize attending to your biological needs by utilizing the restroom or quenching your thirst with a sip of water, nevertheless, please refrain from consuming breakfast at this time. Having a satiated stomach may impede optimal meditation as it can induce diversion of energies towards the process of digestion. Nevertheless, it is advisable to engage in meditation soon after awakening to prevent the brain from receiving hunger signals emanating from the stomach.

Engaging in afternoon meditation can restore your diminished energy levels and enhance your alertness later in the evening. It is also permissible to engage in nighttime meditation prior to sleep; however, it is advised to observe a seated position during the practice. Entering a state of slumber does not qualify as the practice of meditation.

One can also engage in meditation during periods of idleness. Engage in meditation during your journey – this is preferable to prolonged contemplation of unproductive ideas or indulging in recreational activities on your mobile device. Engage in contemplative practice while maintaining a poised stance in a queue, awaiting someone's arrival, or during moments of reprieve. Make idle periods productive.

In times of emotional tumult or unrest, engage in the practice of meditation. This will facilitate the cultivation of a more positive cognitive state. If you are unable to allocate time for meditation, reflect upon the activities you may need to sacrifice or forego. Assess your daily tasks and engagements - you may discover certain activities that lack productivity. Engage in meditation as an alternative to undertaking those activities.

Helpful Attitudes to Meditation

The perception of meditation largely relies on subjectivity, thus emphasizing the vital importance of one's mindset in shaping the outcome. Acquiring the following dispositions will alleviate the challenges you may encounter during the practice of meditation.

Passiveness

One must display a readiness to fully devote oneself to the practice of meditation. If one experiences a state of restlessness, it can lead to heightened tension and an excessive preoccupation with thoughts. The utmost level of relaxation is achieved when one experiences minimal or no mental activity.

Don't try too hard. Allow events to unfold naturally, while directing your attention inward. Engaging in this practice will effectively decelerate the pace of your thoughts and sensations, thereby enabling you to maintain control and resist being overwhelmed by them. This experience will prompt you to engage with your innermost thoughts and emotions, ultimately resulting in enlightenment.

Non-expecting

Engage in meditation for its intrinsic value rather than for any specific purpose or advantage. The mere contemplation of a reward can evoke excitement or induce pressure, thereby detracting from your concentration. Managing one's expectations in meditation can safeguard against disillusionment in instances where outcomes do not align with personal desires. Furthermore, perceiving the activity as an end in itself rather than merely as a means to an end enhances the overall gratification derived from the entire process.

Perseverance

The practice of meditation presents its own set of difficulties, which can, at times, evoke contemplation on whether its benefits outweigh the hardships. Nevertheless, optimal outcomes may solely be attained through consistent meditation. Make the decision to resume meditation promptly and without regard to your emotional state, following any instances of distraction. Acquiring proficiency in this practice will not only enhance your meditation abilities, but also foster the cultivation of your general fortitude and determination.

Positivity

Positive emotions can assist in alleviating the difficulties experienced during the practice of meditation. Strive to maintain a balanced perspective and avoid excessive self-criticism or stringent expectations. Each meditation session is acceptable, provided that one truly engages in the practice. Every session will invariably contribute to your holistic development, irrespective of the outcomes.

Managing Distractions

Engaging in meditation necessitates the allocation of one's consciousness towards the focused object of meditation. Maintain focus and refrain from being diverted, regardless of whether the diversion is enjoyable or disagreeable. Hence, it is advisable to allocate a specific time and designated environment for uninterrupted meditation. Requesting that individuals refrain from causing any interruptions during the session can prove beneficial. Nevertheless, the paramount aspect lies in your unwavering dedication to remain attentive under any circumstances.

When engaging in the practice of meditation, it is possible that external stimuli may divert your attention from your intended focal point. Do not endeavor to engage in conflict with them or eradicate their presence from your thoughts. Do not make any attempts to extend a welcome or offer support to them either. Rather, allow them to manifest and traverse your thoughts. One may conceive of them as ethereal masses that gracefully glide through the celestial expanse - no active intervention is required. You simply need to continue practicing meditation diligently. Should you choose to continue, you will observe their spontaneous resolution.

In lieu of this, you may consider employing a diversionary technique to complement your meditation practice. Reframe your thoughts in the following manner: "Affirm within yourself that with each occurrence of (distraction), you will progressively cultivate a heightened state of (your desired condition)." While this may initially elicit feelings of frustration, perseverance will lead to the gradual reduction of annoyance brought forth by subsequent distractions. You may not even notice it consciously anymore, but your subconscious mind will remain aware of it so that it can work on what you want to happen.

The level of concentration you maintain significantly impacts your performance not only in meditation, but also in any other endeavor. By fully dedicating your focus to the intended objective, interruptions will cease to hinder your advancement. The sole instance in which these interruptions will hold significance is when you permit your focus to indulge in them.

Avoid fixating on an error or a source of irritation. Instead, focus on the process of recovering from the mistake or frustration and proceed ahead. Mitigate disruptions by effectively controlling your concentration.

Meditation As Therapy

The demonstrated psycho physiological associations of meditation mentioned previously serve as robust evidence regarding its advantageous impact on both psychological and physiological well-being. Moreover, while the practice of meditation does not necessarily entail prominent transformations in one's lifestyle, individuals who engage in regular meditation typically cultivate a more optimistic perspective and embrace a more health-conscious way of life. This encompasses the decreased intake of caffeine, nicotine, alcohol, and other over-the-counter medications, adherence to a more nutritious diet with a lower emphasis on meat and processed foods, and the establishment of a more consistent schedule. The origins of these changes, whether they stem from the practice of meditation itself or from self-selection among individuals who choose to meditate, remain uncertain. However, it is undeniable that these alterations significantly enhance the capacity of meditators to effectively manage and mitigate stress. Furthermore, the debate remains as to whether the enhancements observed in individuals undergoing clinical treatment incorporating meditation are attributable to changes in their lifestyle or solely the practice of meditation. Nonetheless, what holds greater significance for both medical practitioners and patients alike is the undeniable fact that there is improvement, rather than the isolation of the precise causative factor behind such improvement.

Undoubtedly, meditation is increasingly being utilized in a clinical context. It has effectively demonstrated therapeutic efficacy in the management of conditions such as hypertension, insomnia, and substance abuse. Furthermore, it has demonstrated considerable efficacy in the management and mitigation of cancer. In its capacity as a prophylactic treatment, it is probable that this approach will diminish the occurrence of the aforementioned conditions, as well as a variety of additional ailments such as migraines, ulcers, cardiac arrests, and arthritis. Enhancements in mental well-being derived from consistent engagement in meditation encompass diminished levels of anxiety, irritability, depression, and neurotic tendencies, alongside amplified states of serenity, emotional equilibrium, and self-regulation. A considerable proportion of psychiatrists and psychotherapists are increasingly incorporating meditation as a complementary approach to conventional treatment modalities. The absence of empirical scientific evidence substantiating the effectiveness of meditation as an adjunct to psychotherapeutic techniques is notable; however, therapists consistently observe a markedly accelerated rate of progress in individuals who engage in meditation. This can be attributed partially to the alleviation of stress and partially to the psychological purification, as elaborated upon subsequently, that ensues during the practice of meditation.

The Process of Meditation

According to a Zen proverb, the process holds more significance than the outcome. In accordance with the aforementioned overview provided at the commencement of this chapter, the conventional objective or 'ultimate aim' of meditation has been the attainment of complete spiritual growth and the actualization of individuals' utmost capabilities. Nonetheless, it must be acknowledged that such aspirations are often impractical and distant for the majority of individuals. Of greater significance is the process of individual metamorphosis entailed in progressing towards this objective - the process of self-exploration and the cognitive, somatic, and affective refinement that ensue from consistent meditation practice.

Typically, the initial outcomes experienced upon embarking on meditation are of a physical nature, characterized by a profound sense of relaxation stemming from the release of bodily tension. This sensation is frequently accompanied by a sense of familiarization, as if one is retracing their steps back to the core of their existence. As your meditation progresses, nevertheless, it may prove disconcerting to encounter undesired thoughts, imaginings, fixations, and assorted diversions intruding upon your consciousness and disrupting your focus. Emotions such as rage and animosity may likewise manifest with considerable potency. Regrettably, a considerable number of individuals become disheartened at this juncture and subsequently abandon their pursuits. Frequently, individuals fail to grasp the fact that this is an unavoidable component of the inner cleansing process.

In the same manner that physical toxins are eliminated through processes like fasting or abstaining from tea or coffee, resulting in undesirable withdrawal symptoms such as headaches, meditation likewise facilitates the release of mental and emotional 'toxins.' This can be attributed to the expression of suppressed emotions, the resolution of profound conflicts, the processing of unresolved psychological material, and similar factors. From this perspective, the outcomes of meditation bear resemblance to those pursued through psychoanalysis. Nevertheless, whereas psychoanalytic techniques are intentionally crafted to retrieve traumatic or repressed events into conscious awareness, meditation, on the other hand, is an entirely organic process that does not involve a deliberate endeavor to revive past experiences. The purification process induced through meditation is not a cause for concern, yet it can pose significant challenges. Undoubtedly, the assistance and guidance of a seasoned instructor play an invaluable role during this phase.

The practice of meditation entails the progressive exploration and elimination of the various layers of conditioning that conceal an individual's authentic essence and obscure their discernment of reality. As preconceived notions and biases are relinquished, an individual's perception of the world and their connection to it grow more lucid. Additionally, as one's faculties of perception and comprehension become more refined, and their ability to focus strengthens, the process of cognition becomes more lucid while stimulating and nurturing creativity.

While it is true that various generalizations can be drawn, it should be understood that the experiences of individual meditators are shaped by their distinct temperaments and requirements. Meditation entails a discrete and individualized journey that gradually leads to a transformation of one's perception of the world and one's entire being.

Methods For Initiating The Relaxation Process

Many individuals engage in the practice of meditation as a means of alleviating the stress associated with their day-to-day obligations. Acquiring the skill of meditation necessitates continual effort, unwavering perseverance, and a steadfast resolve to attain desired results. A substantial number of individuals engage in meditation; however, not all individuals maintain their commitment over an extended period.

In order to cultivate an environment that is conducive to introspection, certain components are necessary in the practice of meditation. It is indeed not overly challenging to engage in its practice. If one is a novice, cultivating an appropriate mindset is imperative for the desired outcome to materialize. Persist in your practice, while exercising caution against excessive self-imposition whenever your mind veers off course. Please be compassionate towards yourself.

To commence, it is imperative to briefly detach oneself from the external sphere in order to initiate the endeavor. Please deactivate any electronic devices or technological gadgets that could potentially serve as a source of diversion. After you have prepared yourself appropriately, you may proceed to undertake the following sequential measures to embark upon your path towards seeking and attaining inner tranquility.

Allocate a specific period for the practice of meditation

Incorporate a dedicated period for mindful contemplation within your daily schedule. It is widely acknowledged that practicing during the morning and evening hours is considered optimal. You can commence your day by dedicating a brief period of approximately 5 to 10 minutes for solitude. Morning meditation typically presents as less challenging due to the decreased mental preoccupations one tends to experience during that time. Certain individuals prefer concluding their day with the practice of meditation. However, the crucial aspect lies in initiating the action.

Seek out a distinct location.

Discovering a serene location is a fundamental aspect of the practice of meditation. One can engage in meditation within the confines of their personal quarters, amidst the serenity of nature, or opt for a leisurely visit to the seaside. Additionally, you have the option to indulge in some melodic tunes, ensuring that the genre selected fosters a sense of relaxation.

Assume an Appropriate Body Position

There exist no prescribed postures to adhere to during the practice of meditation. It is imperative that you ensure your posture is proper, with your back held straight and your head held high. This will provide increased lung capacity to facilitate respiration. Frequently, individuals engage in the practice of mediation by assuming a seated posture, with legs crossed and hands rested upon their lap or knees. However, you are encouraged to select any position that instills a sense of comfort and tranquility. Maintaining a hunched posture will only lead to mental distraction. Additionally, it may be observed that the majority of muscles situated in the upper region of your physique, spanning from the cervical region to the pelvic base, predominantly contribute to the facilitation of respiration by virtue of their engagement with the diaphragm. The mind and body are intricately interconnected. If one possesses a mind that is in equilibrium, it follows that their physical well-being will also be in a state of harmony.

Relax and Unwind Your Entire Body

When experiencing a sensation of tension in specific regions of your body while seated, take the initiative to identify those areas and intentionally induce relaxation within them. It may be necessary for you to modify your posture in order to relax. This phenomenon is typically observed in the musculature proximal to the spinal column. If you perceive yourself to be slightly contorted, strive to align yourself. On occasion, there is a possibility for the facial muscles to experience tension as well. Please proceed to gently unwind your arms and legs, ensuring they do not impede the equilibrium of your upper body. You have the option to place your hands above your thighs, or allow them to hang by your sides. In any case, it would assist you in discerning the components that are misaligned.

Direct your focus towards your breathing

Commence the practice of meditation by engaging in deep diaphragmatic breathing. This method will effectively decelerate your heart rate and induce relaxation in your muscles. Furthermore, it facilitates enhanced oxygen circulation within your body, thereby promoting optimal respiratory efficiency. Pay attention to the sound of your inhalation and exhalation. Direct the scent to travel up your nasal passages, down into your pharynx, into the pulmonary system, and ultimately into the abdominal cavity. Don't judge it. Maintain an upright posture and ensure that your eyes remain closed. Additionally, it is possible to perform this task while keeping your eyes open and directing your gaze slightly downward in a relaxed manner. The main objective is to facilitate the gradual dissipation of the internal noise and mental agitation. In addition, the repetition of a sacred phrase could provide assistance. If you encounter challenges, simply engage in the practice of counting your breath. In the event that your mind becomes distracted, redirect your attention towards it, and gently guide it back while maintaining focus on your breath.

Soothe the Mind

Cultivating a significant degree of receptiveness and tranquility is necessary to calm the mind. This is the underlying rationale behind its reputation as the pinnacle of meditation. Initially, it is possible that one's mind may seem notably occupied, leading to the perception that engaging in meditation only further contributes to its preoccupation. In fact, what you are experiencing is an increased awareness of the mind's inherent busyness.

Develop the cognitive ability to direct your attention towards a singular entity, ensuring the cultivation of mental discipline that leads to the state of mindfulness. Adopting a state of relaxation fosters tranquility and promotes a sense of mental calm. Once your attention is fully centered on a specific point, you may begin to dispel it.

Allow it to pass without passing judgment on its quality. Apply this practice to every thought that enters your mind, until a sense of calmness begins to manifest.

Conclude Your Meditation in a Gradual Manner

Emerging from a state of deep meditation may require a considerable amount of time, particularly when one has attained a profound level of relaxation. It may prove slightly uncomfortable should you rise abruptly. Maintain closed eyes for a brief duration, following which engage in stretching or gentle movements to gradually transition into a state of increased alertness. Upon feeling prepared, gradually begin to open your eyes, allowing the visual stimuli and hues to reintegrate into your perception.

The Dispositions Of Felicity And Appreciation

What is the official definition of gratitude?

Let us commence the discussion by establishing a concise understanding of the concept of gratitude. When someone does something kind for you, it's customary to express gratitude by uttering the phrase "thank you." You've probably heard this expression before. Nevertheless, it is a concept of considerably greater intricacy than simply conveying appreciation for a particular matter.

What is the significance of practicing gratitude?

Whilst we will delve into the specific merits of gratitude at a later juncture, it is imperative to underscore the overarching importance of fostering a sense of gratitude. There exists a substantial body of scientific evidence that substantiates its efficacy, albeit notwithstanding its potential to be perceived as somewhat ambiguous by certain individuals.

Multiple studies have demonstrated that experiencing gratitude can yield a diverse array of favorable outcomes for both an individual's physical well-being and their cognitive processes, emotional state, and interpersonal connections. It instills within us the virtue of acknowledging and valuing the numerous advantageous elements of our existence, alongside the individuals who contribute to them.

Although it may not act as a panacea or a universal remedy, cultivating gratitude can aid us in upholding our equilibrium and fostering a constructive mindset, especially in the face of uncertainty.

A considerable portion of individuals possess an awareness of dissatisfaction, perceiving their lives as incomplete and lacking the things they strongly desire. In such circumstances, it is convenient to juxtapose your own life with those individuals who appear to possess unwavering stability and reach the conclusion that you lack the necessary capabilities. The simple act of nurturing gratitude can prove beneficial in mitigating these emotions.

Does a mindset of appreciation align with all individuals?

It is imperative to engage in preliminary discussion, before delving into the research and evidential aspects pertaining to gratitude, regarding the suitability of gratitude practice for every individual. Despite the abundance of evidence showcasing the merits of this approach, it may not be universally applicable for everyone.

Based on recent studies, it has been determined that every individual exhibits a specific quantity of a characteristic known as "trait gratitude." This attribute plays a significant role in determining the extent to which one is able to perceive and express feelings of gratitude. This level is influenced by a range of factors, encompassing genetics, cultural background, and individual personality traits. The extent to which individuals can cultivate a heightened sense of gratitude remains uncertain; nevertheless, preliminary indications suggest the plausibility of this notion.

Likewise, the eternal quest for happiness can prove wearisome, and existence often presents us with unforeseen moments of adversity at the most unexpected junctures. Despite the numerous benefits associated with fostering a mindset of appreciation, this particular virtue may not be suitable for all individuals. Do not allow yourself to lose hope if you do not perceive any changes, and ensure to raise any apprehensions you may have about your mental well-being with your primary care doctor or another duly qualified medical expert.

The investigation into the concept of gratitude has yielded predominantly favorable outcomes, although a few notable deviations from this pattern should be duly acknowledged. Based on the results of a certain study, it was observed that middle-aged women who had experienced divorce and engaged in the practice of maintaining gratitude journals did not express elevated levels of life satisfaction compared to their counterparts who did not keep gratitude journals. A separate research study revealed that the act of composing and presenting a letter of gratitude to an individual who had positively impacted the lives of children and adolescents potentially elicited a heightened sense of happiness in the recipient. Conversely, this gesture did not result in a corresponding enhancement of personal well-being for the individuals expressing gratitude. The researchers who carried out the study arrived at this particular deduction. This discovery provides support to the notion that cultivating a grateful mindset is an accomplishment that correlates with emotional maturity.

Approaches for cultivating a mindset of appreciation.

Individuals can cultivate an appreciation for their current possessions by engaging in the practice of gratitude, rather than perpetually seeking new acquisitions as a means to attain contentment, or holding the belief that fulfillment can only be attained once all material and physical desires are fulfilled. Individuals exhibit a greater capacity to redirect their attention towards their possessions and accomplishments, rather than fixating on what they lack, through the cultivation of gratitude. This cognitive state also amplifies in intensity through application and training, notwithstanding its initial semblance of being artificially constructed.

The subsequent techniques can be employed on a daily basis to foster an attitude of gratitude.

Draft a formal letter expressing appreciation and dispatch it. One can enhance their level of happiness and cultivate a meaningful connection with another individual by composing a formal letter or email to convey gratitude and admiration for the positive influence they have had on one's life. One can achieve this by conveying their delight and gratitude for the profound influence that individual has exerted on their life. Kindly transmit or, for an enhanced approach, personally deliver it and peruse its contents on-site, preferably, if feasible. Develop a regular practice of sending a minimum of one letter expressing gratitude on a monthly basis. It is advisable to establish a customary practice of periodically composing a letter addressed to oneself.

I express my gratitude to the individual responsible. Do you find yourself lacking the time to engage in writing? Expressing gratitude inwardly could prove beneficial, providing a gesture of thanks to someone who has shown kindness towards you in previous instances. Consider an individual who has provided assistance to you in previous instances.

Keep a gratitude journal. It is advisable to incorporate into your daily schedule the practice of contemplating the blessings you have been bestowed with. You may opt to either document your musings in a personal journal or engage in meaningful discussions about them with a person of significance to you.

Express gratitude for everything that is within your possession. Allocate a portion of your weekly schedule to engage in the practice of maintaining a gratitude journal, wherein you take the opportunity to meditate upon and contemplate the positive occurrences or aspects in your life for which you express gratitude. It can be advantageous to establish a personal objective of acknowledging a specific quantity of items on a weekly basis, for instance, three to five. Make an effort to enhance the level of specificity in your writing and carefully contemplate the emotions associated with any positive occurrences you have experienced.

Pray. Engaging in prayer is a ritualistic act that has the potential to foster the cultivation of gratitude within individuals of faith.

Meditate. The practice of attentiveness in meditation entails maintaining focused awareness on the present moment, refraining from forming any evaluative opinions about it. Directing one's attention towards a specific word or phrase, for instance, "peace," is a common practice observed by numerous individuals. However, one can also adopt a contemplative approach by centering their thoughts on aspects deserving of gratitude, such as the comforting radiance of the sun or pleasant harmonies that captivate the senses.

Sleep Anxiety Management Through The Application Of Directed Hypnosis Methodologies

Clearing Anxieties Held in the Body

Greetings and welcome to this serene therapeutic body scan session designed to assist in alleviating any residual anxiety that may be manifesting within your physical being.

Please ensure that you position your body in a highly comfortable manner, preferably reclined.

Inhale deeply... and as you release your breath, allow your eyes to softly shut.

I would now request your attention to be directed towards the sensations experienced at the crown of your head.

Visualize the arrival of a soothing wave of tranquility, nearing the apex of your head. This state of relaxation effectively dissipates any concerns and anxiety.

Please permit this state of relaxation to transfer gently across your forehead, dissolving any feelings of anxiety that may have resided in this area...

This alleviation eradicates any uncertainty that has infiltrated your mind... perceive your thoughts relinquishing despondency...

Direct your attention to your lower back and acknowledge how it makes contact with the surface underneath. If you detect any sensation of tension in this area, allow a profound sense of relaxation to gradually dissolve it.

Experience the alleviation within your lower torso and hip region... take notice of any feelings arising in connection to fear that might reside within that area. This facilitates a more profound immersion into a state of tranquility, nurturing the process of healing within you... Finally relinquishing these fears completely...

Now, let us retrace our steps along the body in a manner similar to our initial path, albeit with a slight alteration. Envision, instead, the act of drawing in the energy emanating from the earth through your feet. This energy exudes an exceptional depth of affection and possesses a purity that diverges from any previous encounters... Envision this energy to also encompass your preferred hue.

Visualize at present, as the sensation of affection permeates your being through your feet, revitalizing you with renewed vigor...

It ascends from your ankles, meticulously rearranging everything in its path, as this exquisite hue progresses up your legs. It exudes unparalleled purity and delight, ultimately reaching your hips and pelvis, instilling unwavering confidence and a profound sense of inner balance.

Envision the nurturing essence permeating your gastrointestinal tract, yielding profound therapeutic effects...

Visualize it enveloping your lumbar region, imbuing you with fortitude along the vertebral column...

This radiant vitality is enveloping your thoracic region, infusing your respiratory system with fervor... every inhale you draw henceforth is imbued with affection and embracing...

Witness the profound joy that inhabits your heart as it becomes infused with the abundant spirit of Mother Earth...

The influx of revitalizing energy is flowing into your shoulders and extending downwards through each arm, reaching all the way to your hands. Consequently, it empowers you to assume authority over the decisions you make with your hands, guiding every action you take towards the pursuit of well-being and optimal health.

Experience the affectionate energy ascending through your neck and throat, thereby enabling your spoken words to align solely with the authentic truth that resides deep within you. You no longer experience the compulsion to express thoughts or opinions that do not align with your true beliefs or to assent when you do not truly agree.

Your vocal expression possesses exceptional strength and formidable potency, capable of exerting a transformative force on even the most immovable of obstacles.

"Now, allow the nurturing and maternal energy to envelop your entire mind, purifying your thoughts completely...

You have successfully undergone a remarkable transformation today, reshaping every aspect of your being - from the cellular level to the ethereal energies - into a state of pure love and authenticity.

Excellent... You have now become prepared to confront life, unaffected by obstacles that previously hindered you...

Important Considerations While Meditating

It is pertinent to acknowledge that there are a few factors that require thorough examination in order to address them. Let us examine the same matter in order to comprehend the optimal means by which we can derive the utmost advantages from our recently acquired mindfulness practice.

Strategies for mitigating drifting during meditation

It is crucial to comprehend that during the initial stages of meditation, the mind may tend to stray frequently. Therefore, it is imperative to master the ability to restrain such wandering thoughts, particularly considering the limited duration of each meditation session, which is only five minutes. Following is an examination of how we can successfully accomplish this task.

If one engages in closed-eye meditation, it is possible that they may experience a tendency to fall asleep, possibly due to an inadequate amount of sleep received during the nighttime hours. Please ensure that you do.

You experience the 'exertion' of remaining seated. That is primarily attributed to your failure to assume the optimal seating posture. It is necessary for you to maintain a posture with your spine aligned in an upright but relaxed manner. Please refrain from exerting excessive effort to maintain an overly upright posture.

You tend to become excessively swayed by your emotions. It is a common occurrence for unsettling thoughts to arise in one's mind, potentially leading to an inclination towards further exploration of said thoughts. It is imperative to adopt a non-judgmental attitude towards thoughts, allowing them to flow without attachment, in order to promote a serene state of mind and refocus on the fundamental element of meditation, namely, the breath.

Monitoring your advancement in the practice of meditation.

It is frequently observed that individuals may experience heightened levels of frustration due to a perception that the meditation process is not attaining the desired outcomes as expected. It is essential to comprehend that the ultimate advantages of meditation are acquired gradually, yet there exist specific indicators that signify one's progress along the correct trajectory. Here is an examination of those.

There will be an enhancement in the quality of your sleep. You will arise with significantly heightened energy levels and a profound sense of rejuvenation, surpassing any previous experiences.

Gradually, you will attain a heightened state of 'serenity'. When one observes such occurrences, it becomes evident that the practice of meditation is indeed yielding positive results.

If, within a reasonable span of time, you fail to observe these two prominent indicators, it is plausible that your contemplative practice may not be fulfilling its intended purpose. Keep in mind that meditation is a form of practice, implying the possibility of engaging in it less frequently than necessary. Therefore, if you engage in this activity for a duration of five minutes on two occasions daily, it may be advantageous to increase your efforts by performing it four times per day in order to achieve optimal results. It is imperative that you exert maximal effort when undertaking the task. It is not simply a matter of sitting down and closing your eyes; rather, one must diligently strive to engage in the practice with utmost attentiveness and proficiency.

The Emotional and Incitement Mechanisms

Ever since the establishment of psychology, the examination of affective and motivational processes has consistently served as the central focus of every research endeavor and the formulation of psychological theories. Researchers investigate the affective and motivational processes through a multidisciplinary lens, encompassing phenomena expressed through lived experiences, as well as neurophysiological, psychometric, behavioral, and cognitive perspectives. Notwithstanding the various methodologies employed, these processes are regarded as pivotal in accounting for the behavioral dynamics exhibited by the subjects under investigation. The methodologies are strategically implemented with the objective of achieving various objectives across developmental, clinical, organizational, and educational sectors.

Prior to delving into the significance of affective and motivational processes in psychology, it is imperative to initially examine the intricate interconnection between these two phenomena.

Within the realm of psychology, the term 'affect' is employed to denote the emotional state, sensation, or perceptual encounter. The word may have a different meaning in other fields, but in psychology, it relates to the interaction of an organism with the stimuli around it.

The term may also be employed to denote a auditory manifestation, a countenance, or a form of bodily movement that signifies the outcome of engaging with distinct stimuli.

The affective domain constitutes a prominent classification within contemporary psychology, alongside the conative and cognitive dimensions. These three divisions pertain to the conduct, mental processes, and emotional experiences within this domain. Nevertheless, on certain occasions, the cognitive division could be perceived as an integral aspect of the affective division, and conversely, prompting psychologists to deduce that affective processes are constructs of a psycho-physiological nature. According to recent scientific studies, it has been observed that the affective processes exhibit variations within three distinct dimensions, namely arousal, valence, and motivational intensity. Valence pertains to the subjective appraisal, either positive or negative, that an individual assigns to a particular state they have encountered.

Arousal pertains to the quantifiable and observable state of activation within the sympathetic nervous system. This information is also obtained through a self-reporting mechanism. Motivational intensity pertains to the propensity for initiating action, or the inclination to approach or retreat from a given stimulus.

In order for an action to be regarded as motivated, there must exist a distinct impulse urging its execution. The inclusion of these three states in the study of cognition stems from their interconnectedness with cognitive processes.

An individual will respond emotionally to his or someone else's performance in a distinctive manner. An illustration of this can be observed when one obtains a grade of B, which may be viewed positively by numerous individuals, yet for a student initially anticipating a grade of A, the B grade can engender a sense of disappointment. Psychologists elucidate this phenomenon by asserting that the student's disposition, in conjunction with his anticipations, collaboratively engenders an adverse reaction.

Affective processes encompass representative emotional responses and specific temperament attributes. Additional factors encompass the exhibited reactions and sentiments, regardless of their nature, as long as they are intertwined with the emotional conduct, convictions, and cognizance. Affective processes possess the capability to impact the perception and interpretation of cognitive processes by individuals. Emotional processes can likewise hinder, energize, or cease behavior and cognition.

The Operational Characteristics of Efficacy

Throughout history, affective processes have been regarded as diametrically opposed to rational processes. Nevertheless, as additional information has come to light, it has been demonstrated that this classification is erroneous, primarily due to the inherent functionality of numerous affective phenomena. Charles Darwin examined the phenomenon of emotion as a functional component, employing an evolutionary framework for his analysis.

There is a widespread consensus globally that emotions play a crucial role in fostering social interactions and expediting our ability to react swiftly to potentially dangerous stimuli in our surroundings. Nevertheless, research conducted to explore social dynamics in both humans and animals highlights the crucial role of caregivers' formative experiences in fostering emotional well-being for the foreseeable future.

It is postulated that individuals may exhibit varying degrees of affective response towards stimuli, potentially attributable to their respective origins. As an illustration, it is common for humans and primates to commonly exhibit aversion towards spiders and snakes, whereas their sentiments towards flowers and trees are typically positive.

The rationale behind this claim, rooted in the principles of evolution, asserts that humans and primates who acquired the ability to avoid spiders and snakes exhibited higher rates of survival compared to those who did not.

The impact of emotional processes on cognitive processing also yields crucial insights into the characteristics and condition of the surroundings, by discerning whether a particular item or object is favorable or unfavorable. To be more precise, we possess the capability to acquire knowledge regarding the instantaneous worth of both circumstances and entities.

Individuals depend on their emotional responses as a determining factor in assessing the worth or lack thereof of a particular object or concept. The act of making these decisions provides insight into the specific item. This is the underlying cause behind an individual's positive emotions towards something they are fond of and the negative emotions they experience towards something they have a disinterest in. Consequently, due to this factor, affective emotions have served as the foundation for determining the assessments of life satisfaction risk estimates, alongside other comparable evaluations. This is similarly the precise manner in which attitudes are shaped.

Affective cues can be seen not only as the assessments of circumstances and entities, but also as constructive feedback regarding one's performance in relation to a specific assignment. Positive emotions serve as an indicator of achievement, signaling that the current cognitive approach is effective. Conversely, negative emotions function as feedback that signals the need to employ an alternative cognitive strategy to address failure.

Consequently, when individuals are in a positive emotional state, they have a propensity to rely on readily available expectations, knowledge, and heuristics when processing information. A positive emotional state enables the comprehensive reception and assimilation of information.

Hence, affective emotions have a direct impact on the adaptive behaviors, thereby determining the optimal course of action for attaining a specific objective, thus setting it apart from strategies that should be discarded.

The Benefits Of Meditation

The Advantages of Practicing Meditation for Business Professionals and individuals involved in Entrepreneurship

If you have ever endeavored to embark on an entrepreneurial venture, you are undoubtedly acutely acquainted with the arduousness of dedicating extensive periods of time, shouldering increased accountability, and striving to devise remedies for unanticipated challenges. It may be challenging for you to allocate time for practicing meditation in addition to prioritizing the consumption of three nutritionally balanced meals per day and securing an adequate amount of sleep exceeding just a few hours each night.

Some tension is inevitable and natural. However, over time, prolonged and heightened levels of stress can lead to the deterioration of an individual's physical and mental well-being. It is possible that a variety of symptoms, such as recurring headaches, abdominal discomfort, gastrointestinal issues, chest discomfort, sleep disturbances, and increased blood pressure, may arise as a consequence of it. Furthermore, stress exacerbates the symptoms of various ailments and significantly hampers the recuperation process for individuals afflicted with injuries and illnesses.

However, there exists a multitude of benefits that meditation offers to company owners and entrepreneurs. Upon performing meditation, both the body and mind achieve a state of calmness, thereby alleviating the symptoms associated with stress. Meditation enhances the cognitive abilities of the mind, enabling it to engage in tasks of creativity, concentration, and problem-solving with heightened efficacy. Furthermore, engaging in meditation can aid in effectively managing the multitude of information one encounters within a typical workday.

Articulating the rationale behind allocating time from one's demanding agenda for the purpose of engaging in idleness may present a difficulty. Upon closer examination, it becomes evident why numerous corporate executives are inclined towards engaging in meditation, when one considers it as an integral facet of a balanced and wholesome way of life, taking into consideration its manifold cognitive and physiological benefits. By allocating a portion of your schedule to engage in meditation and relaxation, you will witness an elevation in both your overall daily productivity and efficiency.

Moreover, after embarking on the practice of meditation, even mundane tasks such as driving or completing administrative tasks can assume a contemplative nature, as your mind becomes adept at applying the recently acquired state of mindfulness to these activities.

The Impacts of Meditation in the Corporate Setting on Employee Morale

To foster a collective practice of meditation among their employees, certain businesses opt to contract professional meditation services specifically tailored to corporate settings. There are three distinct advantages that a corporation can attain by adopting corporate meditation: enhanced employee productivity, boosted employee morale, and enhanced employee health and wellness.

Due to the potential health benefits of meditation for employees, such as stress reduction, prevention of injuries and illnesses, there is a subsequent decrease in absenteeism costs. Due to the improved physical well-being of employees, there will be a reduced likelihood of them submitting reports of absenteeism. Moreover, employees who hold the conviction that their work is genuinely enhancing their efficiency and well-being will demonstrate greater levels of job contentment, ultimately resulting in a decline in staff attrition.

Meditation is additionally beneficial for individuals whose job responsibilities require the utilization of their creative faculties or necessitate prolonged periods of concentration, including professionals in the fields of engineering, design, architecture, programming, and art, as it enhances productivity. Furthermore, meditation can be of assistance to employees in acquiring new skills due to its ability to improve memory retrieval and overall cognitive capabilities. The capacity of the intellect to concentrate on the subject matter is significantly enhanced when it remains tranquil and devoid of external diversions.

Engaging in meditation can serve as an effective means of elevating employee morale due to various factors. One possible formulation in a formal tone could be: "Firstly, it is worth noting that collaborative engagement in shared experiences within a professional setting has the potential to cultivate a sense of emotional connection among colleagues." Furthermore, the process of relaxation can play a pivotal role in reducing emotional barriers, thereby enhancing the probability of successful collaboration among participants in team assignments and fostering mutual support in the face of tight schedules, high expectations, and dynamic circumstances. Ultimately, the establishment of a corporate meditation program has the potential to enhance employee morale, as it may convey to employees that their supervisors are genuinely invested in their holistic welfare. A corporation that places importance on its employees will make it easier for its employees to experience a sense of pride.

Research investigations are increasingly providing evidence for the benefits of workplace meditation programs. According to Project-Meditation.org, a chemical facility based in Detroit has purportedly implemented a corporate meditation program. Merely three years later, they documented a noteworthy 85% decrease in absenteeism, a remarkable 120% enhancement in overall productivity, a significant 70% reduction in injuries, and an astonishing 520% increase in net income for the enterprise.

Varieties Of Meditation Practices To Employ At Present

There exist numerous methodologies for engaging in meditation customarily influenced by distinct intentions and motivations. Here, we present several illustrations of prevailing practices adopted by the majority of individuals leading a bustling lifestyle engrossed in professional and familial responsibilities.

The requirements of your occupation may result in feelings of stress or anxiety. It is possible that you are currently engaged in a meeting or you are diligently working under the constraints of a specific deadline. There are various strategies that can be employed in the workplace to reduce stress and promote a heightened state of mental clarity. It will assist you in gaining control over the situation and experiencing a heightened sense of tranquility compared to your previous state following the meditation practice. Nonetheless, work is not the sole predicament instigating your distress or unease. Within the confines of this chapter, you shall acquire the knowledge and understanding on the practice of directing your meditative efforts towards a particular issue or situation.

Work Meditation

The concept is rather straightforward. While seated or moving about, it is crucial to redirect your focus promptly towards your breath. The objective is to achieve a numerical count of ten while concurrently engaging in the act of respiration. A complete breath consists of both inhalation and exhalation occurring once. In the event that you find yourself losing track, it is advised to commence the process anew, relinquishing any lingering frustration. Engage in this practice consistently throughout the course of the day to maintain an optimal equilibrium of stress.

The objective of the meditation is commonly referred to as "unwavering focus." This is the designated space where you may direct your attention solely towards a specific object for an indefinite duration. This could either be simple or require dedicated effort. Exerting maximum effort will yield advantageous outcomes in your meditative practice.

Benefits of Work Meditation

One of the numerous advantages of engaging in brief meditative sessions during work hours relates to the enhanced capacity to effectively manage and cope with high levels of stress. Your body effectively acquires the ability to decrease its stress level. Your cardiovascular system will operate at a more physiological rhythm. You will experience a heightened capacity to manage additional tasks and responsibilities. Your level of concentration and proficiency in decision making is heightened.

The advantages of engaging in meditation in a professional setting can yield significant impacts on one's performance and ultimately contribute to an improved quality of life.

Mindfulness Meditation

Mindfulness Meditation is simple. The task is to bring your attention to whatever it is that you may be doing. When engaged in the tasks of painting or writing, it is imperative that one focuses solely on the respective activity at hand.

When engaging in walking, it is imperative to maintain exclusive focus on the activity of walking.

Your mind may appear to meander without restraint. This is entirely ordinary, and it simply entails redirecting your attention back to the task at hand. Even in the event of frequent revisions, it is acceptable. It is a common occurrence among individuals of exceptional aptitude.

Benefits of Mindfulness Meditation

The advantages of this form of meditation carry significant weight. Once you begin to become mindful, then you will begin to notice thoughts and emotions that are harmful before they have a chance to take a hold of you. This meditation offers an additional perk. You will be engaged in your current task, yet you will exhibit heightened mindfulness and enhanced proficiency in exercising mental control by redirecting your focus to its proper sphere.

Additionally, it will aid in decelerating your pace and promoting a state of relaxation. You will be subjected to significantly reduced levels of stress. The primary advantage is that you will not experience a sense of time being squandered. Furthermore, your work will exhibit increased depth and unparalleled profundity.

Compassion Meditation

Compassion meditation entails directing your thoughts towards the circumstances and well-being of individuals in your vicinity. All of the remainder strive for happiness, akin to yourself. Nobody desires to experience sadness or endure hardship, just as you yourself do not wish to feel that way.

Compassion meditation is uncomplicated due to the inherent presence of compassion within oneself. Every individual among us encounters instances of compassion in our day-to-day existence. Moreover, it is the most powerful amongst all sentiments. A mother possesses profound empathy towards her child and is willing to go to great lengths, even enduring personal anguish, to ensure their well-being.

By considering the aforementioned example and bearing in mind that every individual is inherently connected to a familial unit as someone's offspring, parent, sibling, or relative, one will find it markedly simpler to cultivate a sense of empathy towards others.

Benefits of Compassion Meditation

This form of meditation will facilitate the development of a more compassionate and amiable disposition within you. You will ultimately develop into a more adept caregiver, sibling, companion, or even associate. You will eventually emerge as a reliable source of support for others. You will also gain strength and even independence because you have now shifted the focus away from your own ego to be ever so mindful of others. One such prime factor behind the remarkable courage exhibited by soldiers is their deep sense of responsibility towards their nation and its inhabitants. They do not prioritize their own interests.

Commencing The Day & Establishing A Purpose

By firmly establishing our motivation in the early hours of the morning, when our mind is rejuvenated and uncluttered, we greatly enhance the likelihood of recollecting it throughout the day and acting in accordance with that intention.
~Dalai Lama
W
We are all familiar with the sensation of losing track of time throughout the day. Time elapses swiftly, and before one realizes, it is already midday, burdened with an extensive list of tasks and a multitude of thoughts.

Certain individuals engage in morning meditation to cultivate a sense of tranquility prior to immersing themselves in their daily endeavors. Regardless of whether or not I engage in morning meditation, I have discovered immense merit in commencing the day by establishing a deliberate intention regarding what I intend to be attentive towards throughout the course of the day. It serves as an excellent initiation for cultivating a habit of mindfulness, and by day's end, you can reflect upon your progress while embracing self-compassion, regardless of the outcome.

A few examples:

I will maintain mindfulness by focusing on my breath.

I commit myself to displaying acts of kindness towards others.

I will exhibit kindness towards myself.

I will engage in deep breathing exercises in the event that I experience feelings of anxiety.

I will endeavor to engage in a novel experience today.

I will exercise caution and mindfulness in my dietary choices throughout the day.

I am inclined to cultivate a sense of curiosity concerning the state of affairs in the world today.

Exhibit inventiveness in selecting the task you wish to undertake. Ensure that it resonates with you instead of being a haphazard selection. An aspect that you believe would have a notable impact on you.

Regardless of your motive, make it a habit to reevaluate it at least once throughout the day (ideally more often) in order to reinforce your overarching objective. Simply taking a deep breath and restating the intention will suffice. Do not perceive yourself harshly in the event that you encounter difficulty in recollection. There may come a time when your recollection is entirely absent, but even from such an experience, valuable lessons can be derived.

Please exercise caution in regard to your thoughts and emotions concerning your performance. On certain occasions, I make a personal commitment to maintain unwavering confidence throughout the course of my workday, irrespective of any obstacles that may arise. A noble intention. Throughout the course of the day, I might take a moment to contemplate this objective and discern that I am overwhelmed by a sense of discouragement. Perhaps someone has made hurtful remarks which have affected my emotions, or perhaps I have made mistakes that have undermined my self-assurance.

This purportedly does not appear to constitute a triumph by any means, yet there lies a profound potential in the mere acknowledgment of these emotions.

There is a propensity for individuals to adopt a negative mindset when they become aware of their failure to consistently align their actions with their underlying intentions throughout the entire day. However, it is essential to adopt a pragmatic approach, acknowledging and recognizing our initial intent, and understanding that, much like returning to one's breath, it is possible to recommit to our intention regardless of the obstacles we encounter.

Consider establishing a purpose or objective at the start of each day and approach it with a lighthearted demeanor instead of an excessively earnest one. Derive satisfaction from the endeavor and derive satisfaction from the journey of self-discovery as you observe your behaviors and responses throughout the day. Each time you remember your intention, you've automatically entered into a moment of mindfulness and have stepped back to view your day through the lens of awareness.

#6 - Our Parents Reside in Us Forever

We hold an unwavering affection for our parents, irrespective of their attributes and circumstances. And what could be more profound than their continued presence within us, ensuring an unbreakable energetic connection. We possess within us the inherent attributes, characteristics, and conduct inherited from both our maternal and paternal progenitors. Regardless of how much we may perceive ourselves to be identical to one parent, it is imperative to acknowledge that we also possess attributes inherited from the other parent. For instance, it is possible for a daughter to bear a striking resemblance to her father, exhibit nearly all of his behavioral traits, yet also possess distinct characteristics akin to those of her mother. The paternal attributes and characteristics may exert primary influence on her, yet her maternal heritage also manifests within her. Our existence is the outcome of the deep affection our parents share/shared for one another. Their beliefs, qualities, traits, emotional patterns, habits are living within us.

Our existence is owed to our parents, and therefore, we are undeniably a direct continuation of them. They consistently provide in abundance, and we, as their offspring, receive in abundance as well. There are no inherent issues with acquiring additional resources. They bestow upon us this existence, providing us with profound care and fostering our development during infancy, juvenile stages, and occasionally even during our early adulthood. The act of giving and receiving sustains their presence within us. As youthful individuals, it is incumbent upon us to commemorate their existence within our beings, emanating in the manifestation of the Life Force Energy which they have graciously bestowed upon us. Regardless of the actions or personal identities of our parents, there is one aspect for which we ought to express gratitude: the life bestowed upon us by them. It is imperative to acknowledge that we are unable to alter, remove, or make any additions to the intricacies of life, necessitating acceptance of its inherent nature. The vital energy existing within us remains unchanged.

Indeed, it is inevitable that our parents' viewpoints and life experiences may diverge from our own. However, the fundamental essence of existence, namely pure energy, remains immutable for all individuals. It retains its divine essence in an unaltered state. It is possible for individuals to alter their belief system, attitude, and perspective in life, yet it remains beyond anyone's capability to modify or manipulate the fundamental essence of LIFE and LIFE FORCE ENERGY that is bestowed upon us.

Casting judgment upon the inheritance bestowed by our parents results in an imbalance, thereby obstructing the harmonious circulation of the vital LIFE FORCE ENERGY. It is imperative that we bear in mind and recognize the reality that they have bestowed upon us this existence without passing judgment. The union of their love has given rise to our existence, and as such, it warrants utmost reverence and affection. Their alliance is the power accountable for our existence. Assessing the existence bestowed upon us by our parents is akin to evaluating the DIVINE element without comprehending or perceiving the overarching scope or grand design of the soul. As human beings, we often exhibit a proclivity for making snap judgments and offering criticisms based purely on surface-level observations, rather than taking into consideration the encompassing facets such as LOVE, LIFE, Feelings, and Emotions. We typically struggle to fully embrace and accept these elements in their entirety and as they naturally occur. It is only upon receiving that we are able to shift our focus from the mundane and discover matters that hold significance.

The subsequent mindfulness exercise transcends mere meditation; rather, it represents an ethereal journey encompassing one's connection with one's parents and, most significantly, one's embrace of existence itself. This could be perceived as the initial pivotal stage in the process of self-discovery. The process of the soul's progression brings you into closer proximity with your intrinsic essence. I would like to propose that you consider adopting a mindset of personal openness and embark upon this transformative journey towards self-discovery.

Meditation:

1. Please kindly shut your eyes and inhale deeply a few times. Release yourself from the chaos and incessant noise that is occurring within your thoughts. Exhale all of the built-up tension and stress. Simply permit yourself to inhale deeply, directing your focus inward as you release any and all superfluous mental, emotional, or sensory baggage.

2. Embrace the state of centeredness. Inhale tranquility, affection, happiness, and benevolence.

3. Now, envision your parents standing before you. Exhibit profound gratitude towards them for bestowing this life upon us, concurrently demonstrating deep respect and reverence.

4. Allow this occurrence to transpire momentarily, while silently expressing within your innermost being the sentiment, "Mother, Father, I am grateful that you brought me into existence." I express deep appreciation for the

existence that you have bestowed upon me."

5. Experience the vitality inherent in the words you are articulating within the depths of your heart and then allow those sentiments to forge a profound connection with your parents.

6. Convey quietly within your heart, "Mother, Father, I am determined to make a positive impact with the life bestowed upon me." I hold in high regard, demonstrate profound respect for, bestow honor upon, and feel strong affection towards this existence."

7. As you articulate this message, allow the resonance of these words to be sensed deeply within your heart, your essence, and allow this revitalizing vitality to permeate every single constituent of your physical being.

8. I acknowledge, with utmost reverence, that both Mummy and Daddy exist harmoniously within my being, unified and vibrant. The amalgamation of your affection resides within my being."

9. Whilst expressing this sentiment, one shall experience a simultaneous sense of the vitality of existence and the profound connection of affection within oneself. Allow this newfound energy to permeate and intensify within you.

10. After you have assimilated the vitality of existence, simply unwind and compose yourself. Express your appreciation towards your parents and your familial structure for affording you the chance to establish a connection with the vital force of life.

11. Permit both yourself and the newly discovered energies to harmoniously merge. Upon the completion of the integration process, kindly proceed to gradually and tenderly open your eyes.

The aforementioned meditation represents a spiritual journey, a pathway towards embracing existence in its unadulterated form, as bequeathed unto us. It is crucial for us to comprehend that without embracing the vitality inherent within us, our advancement and alignment with our higher consciousness remain unattainable. It is imperative to establish a connection with the vital life force energy in order to attentively perceive the guidance emanating from our higher self or the inner voice within us. In order to establish a connection with this vitality, it is imperative that we convey our sincere appreciation, admiration, and esteem towards the bestowers of this existence - our progenitors. Subsequently, we will comprehend the genuine nature of the vital concept of LIFE. As the act of passing judgments, engaging in criticism, and being driven by ego gradually diminish, an authentic sense of gratitude, profound respect, and genuine love emanate from the very essence of our existence. It is undeniably authentic, serving as a conduit to establish a profound connection with all other facets of elevated consciousness. I recommend allowing these false perceptions of judgment and criticism directed at your parents to dissipate permanently.

Regardless of the circumstances or relationship situation of your parents at the time of your conception, this life was bestowed upon you out of a deep reverence for the vitality of existence. Regardless of their level of happiness as a couple, whether they experienced emotional detachment or were simply filled with joy and anticipation as they prepared to build a family, The undeniable fact remains that they have never passed judgment upon us in bestowing this existence. It was solely an expression of affection. Therefore, it is imperative to comprehend this fundamental principle and engage in the exercise of the soul in order to facilitate more profound rejuvenation. Despite its apparent simplicity, this particular motion underscores the reality that in our rapidly-paced existence, we have grown accustomed to the vital energy that sustains our lives, leading to a lack of acknowledgement or appreciation. As a result of the influence of our environmental circumstances and our limited introspective awareness, we frequently fail to recognize the significance of this time-honored wisdom pertaining to establishing a profound connection with the essence of our parents. This initiative will serve to restore your profound connection with the vital essence of LIFE FORCE ENERGY as well as its providers across every facet of your being. It resembles an intricate process of recalibrating your consciousness to reach the essence of your being, and this advancement holds the potential to serve as your gateway.

Clare's Ten Effortless Strategies For Meditation

Choose the time. Dedicate a daily time frame ranging from three to ten minutes. Commence with brevity and gradually progress. Schedule it in. It is acceptable for the initial phase to require additional time. In the near future, you will discover the optimal duration that suits you best.

2.

Locate an appropriate area characterized by serenity and minimal visual distractions. While adhering to a consistent schedule and utilizing a fixed venue is advisable for fostering habitual behavior, there are instances when one must employ resourcefulness in selecting a suitable setting.

3.

Be comfortable. Wear comfortable clothes. Please ensure that you keep your shoes on or make a decision to remove them.

4.

Discover a suitable posture that affords you ease and relaxation—be it reclining, sitting upright in a chair, assuming the lotus or half-lotus pose, or even lying down in a Savasana position—in order to facilitate unhindered respiration.

5.

Begin by engaging in a guided meditation and simply adhere to the instructions provided.

6.

Maintain a regular breathing pattern or center your attention on your breath. Direct your focus towards the act of respiration, taking in a substantial breath through your nasal passages, and releasing all expelled air through your mouth by engaging your diaphragm. One can even imbibe love and exhale negative thoughts.

7.

When you are feeling unmotivated, remind yourself of the many benefits of meditation. Please record your reason, purpose, or motivation, and make sure to revise it whenever any alterations occur.

8.

Please refrain from concerning yourself with the distractions of your mind straying. It is completely normal. Kindly redirect your attention back to the meditation without experiencing any anger or making any judgments.

9.

Discover a companion for mediation or seek connection within a collective. An acquaintance, partner, or offspring can aid in fostering your sense of responsibility and steadfastness in maintaining your routine. Consider actively participating in a local or online meditation community, wherein you can avail yourself of additional assistance, receive valuable advice, inquire about any uncertainties you may have, or engage in group meditation sessions together.

10.

Celebrate your progress. Express gratitude consistently throughout, if desired (such as by uttering phrases like 'I am thankful for this exquisite sense of relaxation' or 'I express my gratitude for the ease of my breathing'), and, particularly, upon conclusion, when one's improved state is most apparent.

Introduction To Various Forms Of Meditation Suitable For Novices

There exist various forms of meditation. I engage in both of these activities and have discovered them to be highly advantageous for individuals leading demanding lives with hectic schedules. Rather than overwhelming you with an excessive amount of information regarding the various forms of meditation, I believe it would be more beneficial to focus on the primary types. This will allow you to gain a clear understanding of what meditation entails and enable you to select the specific types that align with your lifestyle.

Mantra Meditation

In the practice of Mantra meditation, it is customary to engage in group settings when learning meditation. A teacher shall provide you with a mantra or word that may hold no inherent meaning to you, yet it shall hold personal significance and be customized according to your date of birth and other pertinent factors. Nevertheless, in the context of solitary mantra meditation, one may opt for a profoundly uncomplicated mantra like the universally recognized intonation of "Ommm." This resonating sound, often associated with the persona of Buddhist monks or avid practitioners of Yoga, may sound familiar to your ears. The rationale behind the existence of a word that lacks meaning is to prevent the association of supplementary thoughts with it. Focused attention on this particular word during meditation prevents the occurrence of mental associations commonly prompted by more familiar words. This aids in establishing a solid foundation within yourself. Assuming a comfortable posture, akin to a simplified rendition of the lotus position, one proceeds to engage in the act of chanting a designated word while adopting a prescribed breathing rhythm during the process of meditation. Meditation entails eliminating mundane thoughts, thereby enabling one to derive relaxation and benefits from the practice. This particular form of meditation is well-suited for individuals whose minds tend to be excessively active.

Yoga Meditation

This type of meditation adopts a comparable seated posture, wherein one focuses their attention solely on their breath. Each inhalation and exhalation is regarded as a unit, and as you direct your focus towards the rhythm of your breath, your task is to sustain a sequential count up to ten, after which you begin anew from one. It is appropriate for individuals who possess the necessary level of self-control to effectively segregate their thoughts. This implies that individuals adept at concealing their emotions would be well-suited for this task. I am among their ranks, and I found it relatively effortless to project a courageous demeanor when necessary, despite the persistence of those pessimistic ruminations in my mind prior to embarking on this particular form of meditation. This can be achieved individually or in a classroom setting. One positive aspect of attending classes is the sense of unity and collective purpose experienced within the student cohort, as they strive for enhanced comprehension of life and progression towards individual and collective goals. One benefit of working independently is the ability to have flexibility in scheduling and seamlessly integrate it into one's lifestyle.

Walking meditation

This meditation technique is the third variant that I employ when circumstances deem it necessary. Once you have acquired the necessary self-control to regulate your breathing patterns effectively, you can utilize this technique to restore yourself to a state of emotional equilibrium when confronted with hostile situations or intense arguments. In order to engage in this form of meditation, it is necessary to engage in walking while directing one's gaze towards the ground. This activity is performed with one's eyes open, as it is crucial to avoid any potential hazards. However, one's gaze is directed towards the ground during the process. The concept entails choosing a serene environment for the activity of walking, where disturbances are minimized in order to ensure your focus remains undivided. It is possible that you have observed individuals of a professional nature traversing the premises of the office. It is possible that they are unaware, but they are inadvertently employing meditation as a means to facilitate the resolution of their issues. When engaged in authentic meditation, it yields greater efficacy, particularly in instances where one finds themselves outside of their domestic setting and confronted with unresolved predicaments. Once again, it is imperative to emphasize the significance of incorporating proper breathing techniques. Engaging in this rhythmic activity of walking can offer individuals the opportunity to find resolutions to inquiries that prove exceedingly challenging, whilst channeling their restlessness into constructive movement.

Varieties And Methods Of Meditation

There exist three principal forms of meditation. Practicing contemplative sitting, mindful awareness, and active meditation. Although the categories may not be precise, this classification is as adequate as any other. The primary emphasis lies on Zazen or seated meditation, as it holds the highest level of popularity and is widely regarded as the most effective form.

Zazen

Zazen pertains to the practice of seated meditation, where one remains in a still and upright posture. There exists a multitude of diverse zazen meditation practices encompassing an array of breathing techniques, mudras, and sitting postures, which may prove bewildering for novice practitioners. Our attention can be directed towards the technique that is most practical and beneficial. There exist several essential prerequisites that are crucial for advancing your meditation practice. Prior to commencing meditation, it is crucial to locate a serene environment. It is imperative that there is a sense of tranquility and absence of any disturbances. One cannot simultaneously attain a state of tranquility while harboring concerns regarding potential intruders that may chance upon them during meditation. In lieu of the aforementioned, coastal areas, woodlands, or other natural environments prove to be even more conducive to tranquility, although they are not imperative.

Prior to initiating, make a personal commitment to engage in a daily meditation practice of no less than 20 minutes per day, consistently maintained for a consecutive span of 21 days. Engaging in a personal endeavor for a continuous period of 21 days enhances the likelihood of adhering to this commitment. And the duration of 21 days corresponds to the period required for habit formation, subsequently leading to its integration into one's lifestyle. Although 20 minutes is considered a minimum timeframe, there is some flexibility in this regard. In the event that you happen to miss a day, do not dwell upon it excessively; rather, endeavor to establish a consistent routine for a period of 21 days. Once you have made a commitment, seek out a serene environment where you can engage in daily meditation.

To partake in the practical aspects of the meditation technique is uncomplicated. Assume a vertical posture with a properly aligned spinal column. It may be advantageous for you to utilize a cushion to slightly elevate your spine in order to attain a heightened level of comfort. Assume the Burmese position by crossing your legs (Numerous visual references of this posture can be found on the internet). Alternatively, one may engage in meditation even while sitting in a chair; the paramount requirement, however, is to maintain an upright posture of the spine. Please position your hands in a manner that brings you comfort and proceed to close your eyes. Now, proceed to engage in deep inhalation and exhalation. And direct your attention towards the act of breathing. This technique stands out as the epitome of standardization and one of the utmost efficacious methodologies at one's disposal. Direct your attention to inhalation and exhalation, maintaining nasal breathing exclusively. In the event that you notice your thoughts veering off, a common occurrence, redirect your focus onto the breath. An effective strategy for preventing mental distractions involves reciting a sequence of numbers in ascending and descending order while incorporating strategic pauses at each end point. Specifically, one would commence by counting 1, 2, 3, 4 while ascending, followed by a brief pause of 1, 2, 3, 4 at the apex. Thereafter, the process is repeated during the descent, culminating in another pause of 1, 2, 3, 4 at the nadir. This practice will establish an interconnection with your breath, diverting your attention away from your thoughts. Additionally, this activity is highly soothing and has the ability to alleviate any stress you may be experiencing. Mastering the art of proper respiration and establishing a harmonious bond with one's breath is crucial in fostering tranquility and mitigating the impact of stress.

Additionally, the act of counting aids in the cultivation of mindfulness, enabling one to pacify a restless mind and direct their attention towards the numerical count. Consequently, this concerted effort enhances concentration, regulates respiration, mitigates stress, and cultivates a state of tranquility within the mind. In the practice of Zazen, it holds great significance to establish a harmonious union between the body, mind, and breath, rather than perceiving them as distinct entities. In instances of mental agitation, individuals tend to overlook the significance of proper breathing and instead engage in rapid and shallow respiration. When you soothe one, you will consequently pacify the other due to their interdependence, resulting in the natural harmonization of your body.

There exists a multitude of variations pertaining to the counting technique.

You may opt to inhale and exhale in a natural manner as an alternative. Inhaling fully from the highest point to the lowest point shall be deemed as a single complete breath. Please proceed by systematically counting to ten complete breaths, thereafter commencing anew. In the event that a thought emerges while engaged in counting, it is imperative to duly recognize it and recommence the counting process from the initial stage. It is of utmost significance to recognize that initiating from a starting point of one does not equate to a failure. You are succeeding. Due to the act of commencing anew from the initial numeral, one effectively asserts their authority over the primal instincts of the mind, relying on one's determination and focused mental effort. You are equipping yourself with the capability to direct your mind as desired. To a certain extent, the greater the frequency of your failures or recommencements, the more significant your advancements become, as you persistently reject the inclinations of the mind. In the practice of Zen, this concept is referred to as joriki, denoting a manifestation of spiritual potency. Developing and refining this capability will lead to remarkable advancements in various aspects of your life.

Mindfulness

There exists a notable convergence between the practice of zazen and the concept of mindfulness. The primary distinction lies in the fact that mindfulness can be utilized consistently to bring oneself to a state of awareness and presence in the current moment. While the practice of zazen necessitates meditating in a tranquil environment, mindfulness proves to be more advantageous in scenarios involving work or interpersonal interactions. There exists an extensive array of mindfulness exercises, given the multitude of approaches through which one can cultivate mindfulness. Many individuals display a notable lack of presence and focus during conversations with you, causing them to become easily distracted. One can acquire the ability to be fully engaged and attentive to the present moment by directing one's focus away from external distractions and towards the immediate surroundings.

A prudent practice of mindfulness entails directing your undivided focus towards an object within your surroundings, for a duration of one to two minutes. Therefore, if one happens to be situated within an office space or in front of a computer, it would be most beneficial to allocate a moment to direct one's attention towards an object of interest, such as a pen or a plant, or any other object that may be available. Direct your complete attention towards the singular object, which shall now be the sole object encompassing your current perception. The presence of a natural object can be advantageous, rendering it more preferable. Direct your attention towards the subject at hand and observe its effects, with the anticipation that you may establish a connection or experience profound insights. In a formal tone, it can be phrased as: "At the minimum, engaging in this activity will divert your attention from the monotonous cogitations of a restless mind, commonly associated with the repetition of tasks or fixating on recurring thoughts." The human brain has a tendency to enter into a state of automaticity, continuously repeating certain thoughts or actions, unless one directs its attention towards an alternative stimulus.

Mindful listening can be considered as an additional approach. Engage in the auditory experience of a widely recognized musical composition without any associated branding. Please refrain from fixating on the vocalist, the duration, the genre, or any other aspects of the song. Merely observe and appreciate the music without passing any judgment. One develops the capacity to value it in its essence, refraining from categorizing it based on predetermined notions. One can completely engross themselves in the music, regardless of any preconceived dislike they may hold. This approach offers a means to shift one's focus to the present moment, distancing oneself from the incessant mental activity characterized by thoughts, labels, and conceptualization. This can be accomplished through regular communication with individuals in your daily interactions, liberating yourself from previous analysis, incidents, or perspectives regarding the individual. Attentively attend to their statements and construct your responses based on their discourse. This represents an excellent approach for resolving conflicts, provided it can be effectively implemented.

There is a boundless array of mindfulness variations. One should endeavor to remain mindful of their surroundings and actions, such as being fully present while opening doors, engaging in mindful consumption of food and fluids, or even when performing tasks such as dishwashing.

The essence of the matter is that one can cultivate mindfulness consistently, however, it necessitates establishing specific junctures in one's life where mindfulness will be conscientiously cultivated in the present moment. This constitutes an alternative modality of meditation wherein one abstains from engaging in any form of cognitive judgment or analysis. Instead, the practitioner adopts a state of mindfulness focused solely on a specific object, with no analytical process involved.

What Is Mindfulness?

Mindfulness is the fundamental innate ability of individuals to remain fully engaged and cognizant of their current circumstances and activities without excessive reactivity or being overcome by external stimuli.

While mindfulness is an inherent quality within all individuals, its accessibility is significantly enhanced through consistent daily practice.

When an individual directs their focus towards their immediate sensory experiences or towards their thoughts and emotions, they are engaging in the practice of mindfulness. There is an increasing body of research indicating that the cultivation of mindfulness skillfully reshapes the structural composition of the human brain.

What is meditation?

Meditation is exploring. It does not represent a perpetual endpoint. Your head doesn't come to be vacuumed free of thought, utterly undistracted. It is an exceptional location where each and every moment holds great significance. During meditation, we engage in the exploration of our cognitive processes, encompassing various aspects such as sensory perceptions (such as the feel of air on our skin or the scent permeating the room), mental constructs (inclinations towards affection, aversion, desire, or repulsion), and even imaginative notions (such as envisioning the peculiar sight of an elephant playing a trumpet).

It is important to recognize that within the realm of mindfulness meditation, we are encouraged to set aside our inclination to pass judgment and instead cultivate a genuine sense of curiosity regarding the inner workings of our minds. By approaching our experiences with both warmth and compassion, we foster a greater level of understanding not only towards ourselves but also towards others.

What is the proper approach to engage in mindfulness and meditation practices?

Mindfulness proves invaluable in all instances, be it through engaging in meditation or practicing mindful techniques like pausing and taking a breath when the cellphone rings, as opposed to hastily responding.

Nugget: The Role of Meditation in Safeguarding the Cognitive Decline of the Aging Brain.

Recent studies indicate that engaging in regular meditation practices has the potential to enhance cognitive flexibility and concentration, thus effectively guarding against cognitive decline.

The majority of individuals begin to experience the tendency to misplace their keys, forget people's names, or solve mathematical problems with less ease as they approach middle age. This phenomenon is commonly acknowledged as age-associated cognitive decline. In previous times, it was widely accepted among scientists that this decline was an unavoidable consequence. However, extensive research conducted over the past two decades has unequivocally demonstrated that adult intelligence undergoes changes through experience and education throughout one's lifetime, a phenomenon commonly referred to as neuroplasticity.

Neuroplasticity isn't a given. Epidemiological research indicates that the longevity of the brain is influenced by a multitude of factors including dietary patterns, levels of physical activity, lifestyle choices, and educational attainment. The individual who adopts a more health-conscious and active lifestyle is more likely to sustain their cognitive performance over a prolonged period. Meditation can serve as a crucial factor in promoting holistic well-being and upholding optimal cognitive functioning. The following information presents the current findings from recent research that indicate how the practice of mindfulness meditation can contribute to the preservation of cognitive abilities and functionality in aging individuals.

The Impact of Meditation on Neuroplasticity

In order to maintain cognitive sharpness, it is crucial to uphold the proper functioning of what scientists refer to as your neural reserve. This "reserve" pertains to the cognitive efficacy, capability, or adaptability of your brain. There is mounting evidence indicating that the persistent cognitive training associated with mindfulness meditation may also contribute to the preservation of this "reserve". As an illustration, a review of the evidence has established a correlation between regular meditation and favorable enhancements in cognitive abilities, including heightened focus, increased mindfulness, enhanced memory, and enhanced cognitive performance.

Research indicates that regular meditation has an impact on various states and networks of the brain. The field of neuroscience education focuses on the activation of extensive networks within the brain, which in turn influence a wide range of emotional and cognitive functions. A notable illustration of this phenomenon can be found in a recent study published by a group of researchers at UCLA, wherein it was reported that individuals with extensive meditation experience exhibit higher levels of brain tissue in regions that typically experience age-related deterioration. This suggests that the practice of meditation may have the potential to mitigate cognitive aging and safeguard against age-related decline.

In contrast, brain community training places greater emphasis on enhancing specific cognitive abilities by consistently stimulating a network associated with a particular function, such as attentional control. This can be likened to engaging in a cycle of intellectual exercises that require significant effort and repetition. Both the practice of kingdom coaching and network coaching are widely regarded as crucial components in the pursuit of cognitive sharpness.

www.ingramcontent.com/pod-product-compliance
Lightning Source LLC
Chambersburg PA
CBHW050232120526
44590CB00016B/2057